IF THERE IS A BUTTERFLY THAT DRINKS TEARS

Natalie Damjanovich-Napoleon

IF THERE IS A BUTTERFLY THAT DRINKS TEARS

Image of a Mother Holding Her Baby, Gazing into the Child's Eyes while a Notebook and Pen Rest on a Coffee Table Nearby, 2011

(Materials: ink, breast milk, wipes, baby vomit, dirty diapers, and tea stain on paper)

I try to write
                    the baby cries in rising squawks,
                                                  a chick

                                                         fall
                                                         en
                                                          out
                                                         of
                                                           a
                                                         nest
I want to write
          structure will work: a sonnet, a sestina,
                                              a couplet—the baby
                                                                  sh—
                                                                      its
I will to write
                    my mind is fragment   a sleep-deprived
                                                 baby-wipe on the floor that
                                                missed the trash

I try to write
          why is there no handbook for mother—?
                                          for mothers who write?

I want to write
                    —who has time to read? My breasts leak milk in blotches
                                                    like spilt ink—the earth drinks my
                                                  Rorschach-test message—
                                                                  longing

I will to write
in the stolen moments   nevertheless the gold watch
ticks   gurgles   goo-gahs   cries

I try to write
but I fall asleep on the couch after I collect my
son from day
care
I will to write
for my stories are great and granular   holy and irreverent

epic   and   tiny, significant
and

mundane   as tea leaves'   future tales

I try to write

I try to write

I try to write

I

try

to

write

I

write

to

try

Somehow, I have forgotten the word for

ma—

maj—

ka

mo—

ther and it sits on the tip of my lungs

waiting to be exhaled into life with

lion's

breath

majka = mother (Croatian)

OUT OF THE DARKNESS

THE MORNING AFTER

The morning after
the one-night stand
blame and regret rest
in each palm on
the pillow in equal
measure. The Cure's
'Love Cats' on the pub
jukebox slides in and out
of my mind like a loose
condom. Slipped in my
purse pocket is a card—
a red rescue from
a London phone box—
for 'Pregnancy Help.'
Two pills. Anti-nausea meds.
Motherhood: a decision
I make for myself
on this day, rather than
one that is made for me.

It's Such a Little Thing, This Wanting

It's such a little thing, this wanting.
The tug of a child on a mother's hand to—'Look!'
The heartbeat of a butterfly in a cocoon, witnessed when
held up to the light.
A desire pushed down so deep it becomes a well; hits water.

The following nine erasure poems are created from
WHAT TO EXPECT WHEN YOU'RE EXPECTING
by Heidi E. Murkoff and Sharon Mazel

THE FIRST MONTH

Welcome to your pregnancy!

Maybe it's tender

But

your

body is making to

be you wouldn't expect

around the bend

The countdown to

pinpoint precise

days

o

f

how-

ever

THE SECOND MONTH

spill
the beans
nagging

nipples

can't seem to deflate

you're
a   Sea Breeze
virgin   It's a wild ride

a tadpole

seed—

the

heart   shape   fact,

the first   to be

THE THIRD MONTH

because you woke

you have the strength to lift it

uncomfortable

green olive

kicks

listen—thump thump

THE FOURTH MONTH

expectant

(!)

cloud

energy
pick yourself up

tender

belly

clenched fist—

THE FIFTH MONTH

abstract chance

beginning you will

feel

the serious belly
reality though far

from ready arms

know for sure

THE SIXTH MONTH

doubt moves no
wind
little arms and legs

become visible

finish
line
a light load with

still feet

kick up your sens e s a little

THE SEVENTH MONTH

the biggest stretch

load lugging

labor

Baby

REM

long

blinking

repertoire

THE EIGHTH MONTH

Approximately

expectant

trepidation

tapping into

parenthood—

Your

half gallon of milk

agenda

busy

speaking

little thumb

THE NINTH MONTH

toes … to sleep

last-minute layette

the longest month

the longest

measuring

life on the outside

umbilical

suckle

Here's exciting news:

The Ripening

Hummingbird feather.
Heaving mud swine.
Mother red throat   leaf and vine.
Empty flood birth tub,
front yard buzz-chirp-dive.
Pre-dawn   flutter heart,
unfolding star jasmine vine.

Father father: wither and die—
two years, less than,
from this   my birthright.
Womb pain   hurt   love—
contractions swaddle
animal scent bottle,
endometriosis fault lines.

Birth   woman   active.
Solanas heat. Silence reminds;
sever, cut, hold. Blind
midwife pinch, waters'
slide. Hydrate fear, wonder at the self.
Woman complete, child unseen.
Palm-woven   nest flight.

Ripening cervix opens,
an eye. Howl loba,
the moon's ebb and slide.
Nil by mouth, full in womb.
Push   pain   pull,
tidal burning loom—
cloud fall over mountainside.
Rain   cries   nest
palm   mine.

A Brief History of Western Childbirth

I

As was the way of her people she birthed him alone
beneath the safe umbrella of a fig tree.

The midwives placed a crown of flowers in her hair, whispered
her instructions in the language of the ancestors bled into the patient earth.

Her breath sharp, metallic, yet she knew that long line of women held her.
There was no crack in the father's skull giving rise to a child,

no baby girl found in a stalk of split bamboo.
There was a woman in labor, and heaving and mucus and shit

and blood, time losing all meaning, the Milky Way pushing its light
between the branches and leaves filling her mind with joy and pain.

On her hands and knees there was a feeling like being split open,
a final heave, baby slid off onto a soft mound of grass,

splitting like a head of hair, creating a nest.
Her aunt, many generations back, when the Milky Way

was born had given birth to two sons—
one who made all the good in the world,

and the other who created all evil.
What would this child bring forth? She thought.

II

In time the ancient ways of birth were written over, a palimpsest
of civilized minds, a month of lying in bed before birth,

a will written as the first stitch fell upon a wedding dress,
shrieks for pain relief brought the mercy of the stake and pyre.

Eve made it so: *I will multiply your pains in childbirth.*
You should give birth to your children in pain.

There is hemorrhage and infection and deaths 1 in 3.
The blanket of chloroform's darkness to replace attention and pain.

I dream that pomegranate is sweet with dangerous fragrance, juice
slipping from the corners of Eve's lips and chin, falling to the waiting earth.

The knowledge of birthing ancestors lost, written into the soil,
like lemon on paper, and only one brother survived, the darker one.

Even the Queen of England delivers in twilight sleep,
cold steel forceps replace warm oiled midwives' hands,

more women die.

III

Fogged dreams of returning to the baking of groaning cakes, piss prophets
predicting our pregnancies with a sniff instead of paper strips.

Nostalgia, the forgetting of women's wisdom, replaced by epidurals,
cesareans, lives saved. Yet, like an ancient story written in invisible ink

with exposure to the light, knowledge reappears. Cared for like gladiators
giving birth to the children we adore, allowed food and water

while we birth, a birth plan. Medical science that saves mothers,
babies, only as we allow the voices of birthing women to rise.

The brother of light begins to return to the world, Eve's secret
message appears on the soil, written in the blood of pomegranate juice:

Your pain is your strength.

Return to post-World War II, midwives deliver a breech baby
in a village by the Adriatic, hands tug, turn, slide the baby feet first—

a party perfumed with men's liquor-sweat rages upstairs—
with these hands my own mother's and *baba's* lives saved.

The placenta is buried under a fig tree on a Mediterranean island,
we begin again.

baba = grandmother (Croatian)

The following erasure poem is created from
THE SANDS OF MY LIFE
by Emily Wright

A Birth

You came

        red   gold

              sapphire blue,

                        knowing

on Breastfeeding

Child grows, seed in hand—
now I know how the sun feels
watching flowers bloom.

INTERRUPTED

THE GRAND CANYON AT MIDNIGHT

i 'YOOOOOoooooop' at the depths of Thee,
as deep as where a trickle of water begins.
Divine slash, magnificent infinity, proud stone.

They 'Yeeeeaaah' at you, divine blaaaah, dust and rocks.
Flew to Vegas, took the copter ride:
'Grand Canyon, yeah i seen it. Bloody big hole in the ground.'
Tick.

i yop at Christian minglers, dinos-awe deniers, suburban hat-check lifers.
Helicopter sites, glass sky bridges, canyon hike.
Tick.
i yop with an eon of hourglass sand beneath
feet in my
                    shoes
                              on the ground.

A checklist of sites to loudspeaker about from sites.
Tick.
And my loneliness,
                                   a hole/slash/yawp which cannot be filled
not by the infinite stars i see above me,
lying on the roof of your dead-of-night-blue Mustang.

My yop bounces back from the stars.
Tick.
Was mine the one small yop
                                                       to push us over?

Ghazal to a Mother's Love

The daddy long-legs, a mother, cradles her albino egg sac of blind love,
expectant ceiling corner, hands screech across belly,
expanding balloon love.

Nobody talks about the dreams of forgetting, stroller, baby, keys by the door.
So real I could feel the fur, gnawing teeth—dream of a chimera
too ugly to love.

Singing the cell phone message beep-beep-beep, mockingbird mother
waits in the fig tree, bug broken by her feet, she never forgets
to feed is to love.

My father refused to change a diaper, yet had chicken manure
under farm-blackened nails,
a loss my husband never knew, to care and to change is to love.

My heart is set to burst open, even skin feels compassion for the biting gnat,
the ants hefting toast crumbs. Creatures make copies of themselves to love.

Home, nursing baby in arms, look up—! Natalie, what is that spreading?
A warmth for the constellation of spiderlings I cannot harm;
this is a mother's love.

On Dropping My Favorite Tea Cup After Five Hours Broken Sleep

I feel as vulnerable as a tea cup with a broken handle; as fresh milk left on the countertop in 40-degree heat; as a tea bag, steeped and squeezed of its last drop of liquid; as a piece of ice that has fallen under the refrigerator's warm hum; as a kite heading towards power lines; as a lotus flower in a pond during drought, cracking like the back of an old woman's hand; as a newborn blind joey, crawling across fur into mother's pouch; as a leaf falling into a firestorm; as a lamb born on a farm; as a pen without ink, without paper, without a story to tell; as a mother holding her newborn for the first time.

THE STING OF THE LITTLE THINGS

dishes, breakfast, sweeping, wiping, dishes,
dress myself, brush my teeth, brush his teeth,
toys away, child caught in a net and dressed.
escape to the coffee shop—latte and pastry,
a moment from my toddler-spent house,
my three-year-old in tow to walk away from
the sting of the little things.

two men sit at a table, shirts, ties,
they look important with a capital 'I'.
They stand up, walk away from the table
leave their cups, saucers, plates,
napkins crumpled up. crumbs
scattered like bird feed—

They stride away, their steps
free, assured of their place
in the world, of their place
in the galaxy, even—

a deep, bone-crush weariness envelops.
a sigh escapes. i clear their table, put away the
two cups and saucers and napkins.
coffee and burnt milk linger at the lip of their cups.
i grab a napkin, sweep the crumbs away
into my hand—for the fifth time today.
the sting of the little things

make me feel like a bird feeding off crumbs from a table
when i should feel like a star in the Milky Way.

Raising Demons Among the Savages

a tribute to Shirley Jackson

The house, it escapes her universe.
You are her bubblegum stuck to a shoe,
shards of sand and grass trapped within
a primitive altar offering.
You are her greeting-card-holism.
The catches in the air of abuse,
the other smile of the little creatures
whose actions disintegrate adult minds.
The seeds of dread, a cool cool head.

Sister went off to school.
And she will come home again?

The Contents of My Son's Pockets on Wash Day

One Year Old in his Overall Pockets:

- Half a dozen bruised daisy petals, some torn, others slashed with gray creases.

Two Years Old:

- A toddler handful of dark bark mulch.
- A piece of black pipe cleaner twisted into a hook, or is it a question mark?

Three Years Old:

- One brown wooden bead.
- A beheaded white everlasting flower—no stem intact.
- Three white sticks, each about an inch and a half long.
- A Lego-man's head.
- A plastic scorpion, with pincers and a tail, painted brown on top, pale on the abdomen—real enough that I flinch when I pick it up.
- A Lego-man's head.

Four Years Old:

- A plastic sunshine bear, the kind that fits on the end of a pencil.
- A popsicle stick wrapped in gold pipe cleaner.
- The chewed remnants of a burst yellow balloon—*Oh my god, he could have choked!*
- A plastic amber jewel, shaped like a teardrop.

Five Years Old:

- One large, red glass bead.
- A teeny tiny pine cone seed.
- A Lego doctor—without a head.
- A rectangular piece of clear mosaic glass.
- Three brown tree twigs, each around an inch long.
- A clump of kelp roots twisted around a rock.
- A round seed with lines on it, scribbles like snail trails.
- A black rock, big enough to fit into a five-year-old's palm.
- One piece of white string, no knots, three inches long.

Six Years Old:

- A blue rubber T-Rex, one leg lifted, ready to pounce.
- A smooth quartz rock, the shape and size of a child's baby canine tooth.
- A one-inch diameter rock—*no!*—a sand coloured ball made from a compressed napkin found in a pocket, washed then tossed and dried into a paper ball.
- A hand-drawn Pokémon character, made on green paper, drawn with a blue marker. My son's six-year-old hands have cut out the shape of the character—did he get help?—with enough care that he's stayed outside the blue lines. A vertical crease in the paper across its mouth makes it look like the Pokémon is smiling.

Following the Discovery of a Rotten Banana in his School Backpack Pocket:

- Lego man handcuffs.
- A heptagon of paper clips.
- A black rubber toy car tyre.
- One shiny, untarnished brass penny.
- A rectangle of black cardstock folded in half.
- A crayon rubbing of a woman with long hair, wearing a bikini bottom, body cut-out like a paper doll.

On His Last Day as a Six-Year-Old:

- The exposed chassis of a Hot Wheels car, four wheels attached, two bent inwards.
- A length of dark green yarn entangled within five or six dead daisy heads.

Conjunction

when you picked your first piece of fluff off the carpet with your fat b
when you made your first joke, repeating back our baby babble
when you first cried out 'Mama' in the night
when you made those faun-like early steps
when you kissed my owie better for the first time
when you played 'Ab-cabba-dabba' magic reveal
when you spun around the kitchen chiming, 'Spinning, turning, dib
when you made up your first song 'Orange Car Knocked the Bri
when you first spoke to me on the phone, your voice sounding shrun
when you did your first toddler run & leap into my arms
my heart broke open—cr

ıgers

bby'
ver'
ıd far away
ıis is when
y crack

Woman

after Woman: A Celebration *by Peter Fetterman*

We weep for you when you die in your wars,
we hang our heads, bury you in our arms, we wear veils, we bury ourselv
we get fat and old and happy, and drink and laugh, heads thrown ba
we tend to roses in a window vase, chenille curtains, light and shado
we stare at waves alone on the shore, hand-woven reed basket in arms
we flee a dust storm, both hands grasping white school hats, eggs
we dance in circles, skirts marking grooves in the air, we spin like reco
we bake bread, fry frites, grin at the beauty of a song,
we lose our skirts on the roller coaster at the funfair, when towers fa
we wash ourselves in a basin in Provence, worn shuttered windows, nake
we nurse our children hidden from view,
we kiss our lovers goodbye at train stations, wave, stand alone and wai
we investigate mirrors and braid each other's hair,
we walk through mountains boom box in hand, flowing skirt swiping t
we stare out windows, in silhouette our heads turned away, cut off fro
we sit under sun-bleached steer skulls grasping dead tree logs,
we bend our knees and confess to priests as if we are lovers,
we hold up the clouds and the sky with our hands,
we pick apples in orchards,
we crack pomegranates open.

ve,
sty and full,
tering through,

enage heads,
ayers with sure needles,

grasp each other and stare out windows at the flickering lights,
afraid,

ads of dead flowers as we trek by,
ew,

IN MOTHERHOOD A KIND OF MADNESS

Day after day wallpaper sheds layers, reveals a kind of madness,
life lived through a child's laughter and joy.
The house a Hall of Mirrors, dead ends, distorted images;
the wallpaper drives me mad, where does the pattern start?

Life lived through a child's laughter and joy,
to find my own joy, my one art—there's disaster.
The wallpaper drives me mad, where does the pattern start?
Where does it end? This life cannot be my beginning.

To find my own joy, my one art—there's disaster.
My mind whirled in a Gravitron, stuck to walls, immovable—
where does it end? This life cannot be my beginning.
Beside my wailing child on the carousel, a spectator spinning round.

My mind whirled in a Gravitron, stuck to walls, immovable.
Women crawl and shake inside the wallpaper, climb through free.
Beside my wailing child on the carousel, a spectator spinning round,
peeling back paper, strip by strip, 'til bare walls revealed.

Women crawl and shake inside the wallpaper, climb through free.
In the pattern I've lost the outline of my country, my father, my keys.
Peeling back paper, strip by strip, 'til bare walls—
Day after day wallpaper sheds layers, beginnings.

the Crackle

In the bitter morning I tell my son to wet and comb the 'cocky' on top of his ryegrass-blond hair. And I don't know if that's Aussie slang, or if my dad flung his head forward and back, then shook it out of his bilingual beak. My son asks me, 'What's a 'cocky', Mama?' And I tell him, 'It's a galah.' A bird gray, with a rose breast and crest, squawking and chiaking us at every turn. The crackle, a swinging gray cloud in one direction, pink in the other, like a West Australian sunset on the underside of a cloud. When I was a kid, my aunty left her cocky with us when she went on holiday. The bird learned to screech my brother's name to the sound coming out from between my mother's gritted teeth. My mother didn't need to drop the bird in its cage down a mine shaft and whisper words to teach it to speak, like Ed in Katharine Susannah Prichard's 'The Galah.' In her story the 'pink parrot' never spoke a human word, knowing how love can clip our wings, leave us repeating back sounds we don't understand, each of us hearing a different language.

He says, 'Obama'

He says, 'Obama'
when we ask who
the president is.
He is three and says
the president's name,
points, beams at us
as if he's seen
a bird in the sky when
Obama appears on TV.

There is that thing
with feathers in the air.
I recall the day at
Farmer's Market
in Santa Monica
after Obama was elected.
So many heads held high,
wide smiles, the January
grey became blue, electric.

Then, we thought hope asked
nothing of us. How wrong we
were, those crumbs demand
to be followed, to be
collected by hungry birds.

We Will Not Speak His Name

December 14, 2012 (Santa Barbara, USA)

You wake up. You wake up and you think you know, *today will be like any other day.* You wake up, but before you do it's time for the 5:00am pre-dawn dance with your two-year-old, crawling into bed with you and your husband. Broken kick sleep. A little arm wrapped around your neck in a toddler chokehold. Nuzzling. Golden light. Blinds. Perfect stripes of sunlight, eyelids you do not want to open. You wake up, but before you do, he tries to make butterfly kisses, pressing his face and eye into your cheek. These are not butterfly kisses, but you don't care. 'More more,' he says. You wake up, but before you do it's the questions, 'Fire in sky?' 'Yes, that's the sun.' 'Burns?' 'Only if you get too close.' You wake up, turn on the TV, *20 children and 6 adults have been killed in a mass shooting at a grade school in Newtown, Connecticut …* . You wake up. Toast burnt, scrape. Jam, peanut butter. 'Triangles please, mama.' You stare out the kitchen window at the rising sun—today it is fogged over, distant, struggling to climb.

for the victims of the Sandy Hook Elementary School shooting, 2012.

if There is a Butterfly that Drinks Tears

If there is a butterfly that drinks tears
let it drink the tears of mothers. Down South

great walls begin to spring up between butterfly
preserves at the speed ice sheets break

off in Antarctica. Monarchs fight to
find a place to overwinter. Target holes

in their wings, a ragged curtain left hanging
in a house too long. If I step off this path

and crush a butterfly underfoot will my
misstep ripple through time?

On the siding of our cottage, my four-year-old
spies a chrysalis. In the high overhead

light we observe the translucent veil between
two worlds, the pulse of a heartbeat, the stained

glass window outline of wings.
There are 'ooos' and 'aaahs.'

With two sticks in hand my son plays crocodile and
whacks the chrysalis, splitting it from the cremaster.

I scream, 'No!'
Insides turn to liquid.

The turtle does not turn her head, she
plods on, a map of the Milky Way carved

onto the shell she carries on her back.
If there is a butterfly that drinks tears

let it drink the tears of children who do
not understand their mother's anger. I pick

up the chrysalis from the ground, set it on a
warm ledge and hope for the best. I try to

explain action and consequence to my
four-year old, but to him there is only

the action and reaction of an impassive,
amoral toddler-dictator. The caterpillar digests itself,

turns to liquid inside the chrysalis before it is made
into a butterfly. In that soup there are cells that

survive this process; imaginal discs.
These cells hold onto a memory of what

they are to become. How do we remember who
we're meant to be? A sip of salt, imaginal discs,

a scatter of minerals, infinitesimal elements in a
stew that keeps us alive. In the Amazon,

Julia butterflies drink the tears of turtles;
the sweat of animals; humans,

and given the chance, crocodile tears, too.

The following erasure poem is created from
TRUMP'S EVOLVING WORDS ON THE WALL
by Ron Nixon and Linda Qiu

on Day One, We Will Begin Working

The Wall is the Wall

a wall, a real
wall.

build a wall a great wall
big beautiful doors

openings in that wall

a wall

borders barriers the wall

the
southern border, lots of sun, lots of heat the wall

a solar wall

a big, fat beautiful door the wall

a wall
walls

the wall

a wall
a great wall,

a crummy wall a wall
beautiful door

a wall? a fence? a wall?

the Great Wall

the wall. The wall's
a wall.

a wall
any wall

On the fence— It's a wall.
build a fence

climb over

the wall will be
'beautiful.'

THE LABYRINTH AND THE THREAD

after Theseus and the Minotaur *by Antoine-Louis Barye*

I hate you, I hate you, I hate you …
Before the first 'I hate you,'
I thought my heart would crack,
into a thousand puzzle pieces
like the three boxes of crockery
I shipped from there to here,
my other life laid to waste.
Hot loathing, memory
tumbles
out of these words
and echoes in the chamber
of the labyrinth, bouncing
off corners and diffracting,
breadcrumbs left in a forest.

I try to follow the skein out of
the labyrinth in the dark, grope
my hands outwards, tug a whisker,
let go, touch the prickled skin of a man,
the ridges of a horn, a wiry tail.
My fingers stick together, I lick.
My tongue tastes metallic,
cut on the blade of Aegeus.
Somehow, in the dark, it never feels
like I am getting from here to there,
though I cling to the thread,
spiral webs of silk stick together,
entangle, a signal line with no
return message.

The Minotaur cries out
to his mother, gropes, falters,
tugs at the thread as he exhales
a whisper with his last cloud of breath,
I love you, I love you, I love you …

I hear nothing but my echoing footsteps
stumbling on cobblestones. I see light,
feel cool air at the back of my throat.
I am a thread returning to the spool.
I love you, I hate you, I love you …

Phantom Pregnancy

for Sonia

I feel something flickering inside me,
light entering a filament,
tugging at my uterine tendons—
dot dot dot, dash dash dash, dot dot dot.
Butterfly wings touch the insides of my belly
and I want to giggle and shriek with the
delight and archetypal wonder of it all.
Smells repulse me; dog urine at one hundred paces,
manure in garden beds a waste-treatment plant,
perfumes and scented oils once adored making
me heady and dizzy like a swooning debutante.
My breasts blue-veined, ready to fill.
Then it starts, the backflip heartbeats in my womb,
the grandfather clock's pendulum swings,
like a glamorous trapeze artist in a circus,
all feathers and sparkles and smiles.

I check my calendar for alabaster appointments,
forgotten Egyptian busts, too pure, too perfect
to be real. The dates, the dates … I'm not sure—
tick-tock click-clock ding-dong dot dot dash—
At the ultrasound the technician looks at me,
calls the doctor in, pauses, and in the time
it takes to draw a breath I pray ten times
and make a deal with God to be Good.
On the screen; blackness, no ghostly shape,
no beating heart, only my name at the
bottom, blinking, a Radium Girl's smile,
glowing chartreuse, missing teeth.

This is the limb I grew when the other was lost.
What a terrible and beautiful thing grief
can sprout; beating and flickering
and tugging its way in. The clock's
pendulum continues to swing,
a glamorous trapeze artist in a circus,
all feathers and sparkles and smiles, smiles, smiles.

Heartbeat

At the cafe, after the abortion, I ask if you're okay and you say you feel fine, a bit of heavy bleeding. You have a pad on because you can't use a tampon. 'Risk of infection' they told you at the clean, white clinic you were out of in thirty minutes. We talk about how you can finish college now and get a job as a journalist like you'd always planned. We laugh at an article in a magazine left open on a table nearby that reads 'How to Be the Girl You've Always Wanted to Be' beside photos of the same girl typing, gardening, curling her lashes, doing yoga, twirling her skirt. You and your new boyfriend had only been dating a couple of months, he didn't pull out when he was meant to, coming into you instead, making this bloody mess you had to deal with. He stayed with you and held your hand. Many years later, still together, you had three kids, a good relationship, a mostly happy life. You never had to think about whether drinking a bottle of castor oil or using a knitting needle to puncture through your cervix would work. You were never given the burden of having to ask that biker friend of a friend if they knew someone you could hand an envelope of money to in a grimy room off an alleyway to give you a chance at your own life. You never had to deal with a heartbeat law that says the heartbeat of a cluster of cells in your womb is more important than your own living, breathing, thinking, feeling human heartbeat. We sat there over coffee and held hands and cried together for the life you could have been forced to bear, for the promise of life you lost, for the mistakes we all make. We wept for bad timing and the women before you and I who had died in desperation trying to preserve their own heartbeat, their own chance at life, instead of being vessels for the mistakes and laws of men.

Endometriosis is Not a Metaphor (a Sestina)

There is this *thing*, this *thing* that lives inside
me, it begins as a bundle of blood,
a prisoner with a shank in hand, tendrils
fighting to escape the lock-down.
This pain is personified danger,
jellyfish stingers, swinging hysteria.

The frisson of Gilman's hysteria
expires within the psyche of my uterus. Inside
the wallpaper of my mind pain-scale danger
swirls from yellow to amber to red—moon-blood
patterns define me. My dis-ease morning glory tendrils,
purple bruises; mad fingers trace the motif down.

Metaphors for girls abound, I am a butterfly larva, tendrils
seeking out a way forward on the leaf, free of the hysteria
of red versus green. Unknown years, traps down
below, left me strangled by my endo growth, gripped inside
and out endo cells cannot bind enough blood.
Butterfly wings press against swollen belly, sprout 'Danger!'

A decade of doctors consulted, delivered Little-Girl-No-Danger
lectures, patted me on the head, and said: Tendrils
don't grow outside the womb, take a pill, lie down, the blood
is only eight tablespoons, girl who became the hysteria
of woman too soon. The pain women feel inside
isn't real, remain silent, unseen; prepare for the letdown.

Quackery began with Greek fear of roaming uteri, driven down
to suffocate. Vaginas sniff the good smells, sneeze! Danger
of sexual fluids, healing of paroxysmal convulsions—*Oh inside*
surrender! Freud told us of our scar, grasping like tendrils
to seek a penis. The cure: get married, have babies, twist home into hysteria,
stare out the window over the kitchen sink; coax our unmanageable blood.

But the devil is in the women's troubles and he's bloody
with the barbed wire of blame; the Hippocratic Oath he broke down.
All the time wasted being told my body lies, but truth buried hysteria
deep, 6 x 6 x 6, in the silent place where she resides. Got danger
money for doing the labor of ten men who couldn't fix me with ten drills,
ten screws or ten surgeries. The flap of wings echo on my insides.

When the Plum Tree Fruits I Think of You

It starts with the bloody pulp of
plums fruiting early that year—
our house being tented for termites,
the flowers I left in the vase
shriveled like dehydrated fruit—
the flu that filled my head with khaki snot,
then tricked the endometriosis
and my immune system—
the plume of soft jellyfish in the water
where we snorkelled in Florida—
the visit from my cousin in Newport Beach—
the early ultrasound I insisted
on at the OB-GYN—
not being able to talk about 'It'—
the one-year anniversary of
my father's death, which became
another anniversary—

It starts with—
all beings that draw
breath must live and die.
It starts with two gametes, a zygote,
dividing cells. A mother's 'instinct'—
a miscarriage, blood thick and deep red
as a plum split open—

Unborn

The butterflies
and the bees
and the hummingbirds
are mocking me

dancing and flitt-er-ing and
twittering by my bedroom
window, in my garden,
on campus, where I
work, by the bushes,
where I
park my car

And when I feel most dark
they frighten me with
a ‘tzt … tzt … tzt’,
and I start
like a rabbit
back
to life

Maybe they are mocking me
because I am too human,
too dark,
too weighed
down to see
the benefit of lightness,
of an eight-and-a-half-week life span—
to take joy in and
savor the movement of
the earth around
the sun
the sun upon my face
my face into the
ocean breeze

Maybe it
        (no, not 'it', '*the* baby', '*my* baby')
decided
being a human was
too heavy an existence and that
being
lighter than a penny
would outshine
a life of unflinching
unrelenting
spinning
around the sun
tens-of thousands-of-who-
can-keep-count
times

THE PUNCTUATION OF INFERTILITY

! [the first year]
!? [the second]
— [the third]
... [the years in between]
X [one year after my father died]
; [the fifteenth year]
/ / [how I learned to live with it]

Breaks

If all of this
br—
eaks,

cr
a
cks

off

at the San
Andreas Fault
and collapses
into the
Pacific like
the dynamited faces
of the Buddhas
of Bamiyan,
I will know
I have lived with
the
privilege
of being
your mother;
the first for nine
years, the second
for ten weeks.

If not,
next time we
pass James
Dean’s crash site
I will blow a
kiss to
impossible intersections,
impossible angles,
impossible death.
And wish that
kiss lands nearby,
at Cholame,
where
I’m told,
the fault line
and the
highway
meet.

TIME IS NOT AN ARROW

Night Blooming Cereus

after Night Blooming Cereus *by Sally Mann*

Family: *Cactaceae*
Genus: *Hylocereus Undatus*
Water: Regularly until flowering commences

Passed down from mother to daughter, friend to friend
this blood moon eclipse reflects in the waxy shadow
of my cup of tea, an oxidized lunar sky. Milky clouds drift
across the tea's surface revealing to peoples, ancient & present,
the moon moves beyond the edge. She is a great sphere, returning
the Earth's light back to us each evening as an act of love.

The shadows of youth move across the moon, clinging
to the bark of a tree, the siding of a house, the nearest bare wall,
the flat chests of boys and girls and those in-between
with roots that breathe globules of wet air.
Once flowering each bud remains luminescent for one
night before withering into a dancer's full-length skirt.
Spent blooms hug the neck of childhood,
a wounded swan seeking solace from the sins of men.
In the deep South, the Queen
of the Night may flower all summer long.
Water sparingly once blooms appear.
Origin unknown.

What Little Girls Are Made Of

If I am good.
If I am *goooood.*
I'm told all the good
things will come to me.
It has been this way for millennia.
On my feet or on my knees.
I could be the best
little girl you want me
to be. And I try, and I try.
Like a shell
found on the beach,
bleached clean, Pantone Bright White—
spiraled inward—
symmetry.
Perfect. The enemy of—

I am waiting to be.
I am waiting to be
filled with your
expectations. Your
grace. Your
signs. Your pink lace
ruffled dreams. Your
sweet and nice. But
not the spice. Not
the spice.

Born of Woman

'The body has been made so problematic for women that it has often seemed easier to shrug it off and travel as a disembodied spirit'.—Adrienne Rich

Your first home was a woman, and since your conception
You woke, fighting to find your way back to the ocean.

Spirits call, women gloaming above the commotion,
Without bodies salt cannot take us—siphon the ocean.

Bodiless you wander, you rage, unheard premonitions,
Pen in hand, rake in hand, you plough words into the sub-ocean.

Sirens call on the rocks, voices ghost-fabric fine-spun,
Fisherwoman cries, 'Never turn your back on the ocean.'

On my knees, child gone too soon, within the womb countermotion,
A fetus, amniocentesis, withdraws back to the ocean.

I am not a child, I am a woman, human, born in devotion,
My body, problematic, blood like gravity pulls me back to the ocean.

Bodied, disembodied; we are forever unfolding in forward motion,
One experience we all share, bodies growing within a woman,
within an ocean.

THE NIGHT IS MORE

'Night is not less; it's more.'–Jeanette Winterson

My God! What a terrible and beautiful place this world is!
And then the night closes in and I bleed for 25 days.
25 days—who can bleed for that long and survive?
A woman. A woman can; and the night
is terrible and dark as wine, it is viscous blood,
beginning to turn from red to chocolate
to black as it cools and thickens.
And I wouldn't bother so much about being a woman
except your hating makes me embrace it more.

My God! What a terrible and beautiful place this world is!
And then the night closes in offering more.
The night my mother, with the limitlessness
of distance and arms that wrap me
in an amniotic embrace as only a mother's can.
Mother: from a child's first breath,
giver of life and bringer of death.
How can I even be standing before you today
saying these words? Writing poetry in the bath naked,
foot over my knee in a number 4, the hanged, drowned
woman. How can I still be here when I have suffered
this litany of indignities thrown forth at my self?
Like the cockroach found tracking across the kitchen floorboards
with a switch of the midnight light.
Like the flickering of bat wings under a highway bridge
in Texas. Like a city in blackout, invisible men
in trench coats and Fedoras moving furniture
while we sleep. Each assault a razor blade cut
to my birth in caul, and the skin of glass
that contains my humanity. Then the night closes in
and offers more, so terrible and beautiful.

My God! What a terrible and beautiful place this world is!
After light the night follows. Pulses. Stars inhale; exhale.
Then the night, with the arms of the goddess
of the evening sky, Nut, embraces us
and we stick together—fingers on a hand
touching a pool of blood.
Because she does not ask me to be less than who I am.
Because she opens the door.

Time is Not an Arrow

Time is not an arrow
and I am neither a dog,
nor a wolf, yet both
reside in me. In the dream
I am both within and outside myself,
and time bends upon itself
a spinning Celtic spiral,
turning from black to white to gray;
set to hypnotize. I ask myself:
Did I feed the wolf, the dog
or the little girl within me?

The twilight creeps,
a bank of marine layer
hugging the coast of my
memory. In dreams I have
spoken to the dead, worn
my baba's cream satin dress,
hugged my father and smelt
the rust of his sweat, met
with the confusion of spirits
as they pat their sides, put their hands
in their pockets and wonder
at the loss of their corporeal
existence—as if it's a wallet
to be found and returned.
When I try to reassure the dead,
everything is okay, all I am left
with is a palm-full of water
that I stutter to explain is melted ice.
In this place, time is like a planet
without gravity which can hold
nothing down.

Once, I had a vision that my entire life
was held in the palm of another
as she sat, cross-legged, black braids
over her shoulders staring ahead,
dreaming my life into her hands.
The gossamer thread of
eon's web connected us.
During the length of her vision
I had lived my entire life.
The girl has eaten the dog
inside me and become a wolf.

My eyelids, so heavy in
the dream last night they felt
like they had been Scotch-taped
shut. I work in a store and sell vintage clothes.
Then get lost between the maze of racks
looking at thrift store threads,
until I remember the rock maze at
La Casa de Maria. I place one foot in front
of the other in a moving meditation,
as oak trees spring up underfoot,
my feet roll over acorns, trip over piles
of discarded clothes until I find my way out.
In the gloaming velvet light, my lids
are as heavy as bats' wings
and I cannot tell if it is a dog
or a wolf before me. I try to feed
the beast before it eats me to sleep, yet, before
I can, time bends flat and round and shiny
as a Vantablack vinyl record,
absorbing all visible light.

One day I will meet you there
maybe we are already in that land together.
Look at your feet. Do they stick to the ground,
or float above? Shhhhhhh
of a needle stuck in a groove—
we are here.

Night Stitches (a cento)

At this hour the men all look
as if they'd never had mothers.
They do not   see me. I bring the cups.
I bring the silver. The dark itself not dark enough
but needing to be added to   handful
by handful   if necessary.

The night has cut each from each
and curled the petals   back from the stalk.
'The poets are fools. They   read
only
          in   fragments.'

The stillness chained by
wrinkled darkness   strains
throughout the Universe to be free.
Mother, I write home, I am close,
and   give me my body back.

Hear, how the night becomes
thinned-out and hollow.
Night like a fling of crows
disperses and is gone.

One night might come upon me like a
doorless cage while I sleep,
soul and body
constructing each other after dark.

And poetry of the night
and the witness in shadow,
in dust, in   Nothing.

O the Celestial Objects

brighter celestial objects

refer

the naked

will

to

a dark locatic

light

that surrounds

You will see eyes

outside

the sky

map

cellophane

moonless nights

void

sion

Syzygy

for Brett

You play the spoons on your thigh, I play
the knives, beating them against my chest like fists.

I watch the moonrise, a lenticular spotlight over New York,
you wander the desert, Mojave, giant sand, nuclear lens landscapes,

a Cold War Geiger counter, images moving needle-like East and West.
Inside I am a whirly bird, flailing in never ending circles,

you are a slingshot, catching the wind.
Yet, somehow, we are yoked together.

And I don't know if you pulled me, or if I am pulling you,
maybe this is the backdraft drawing us back together or flinging us forward.

I imagine all that humanity has done, good and bad, has drawn us together,
and our son is the syzygy of the Moon and Earth and Mars.

The hour between the wolf and the dog is calling and I must go,
coyotes yip and cackle in the desert, my eyelids are heavy, your lips numb.

It is time to fall asleep and rise together in the silent eclipse of an atomic sunset.

If You Were to Say to Me the Words I Wanted to Hear

You would tell me that giving birth is like climbing a mountain solo, and that you are as proud of me as Joan of Arc's mother was of her, for facing the flames. You would say that love for your baby comes like a flood, then swallows you whole before you can find yourself again. You would tell me I have a rebel heart, and to cradle it like a newborn through motherhood, to not let it wither and die. You would tell me that having a child is like ripping the beating heart out of your chest and letting it go in the world. Letting it go, and hoping it comes home each day safe and alive, yet knowing it will not return undamaged. You would tell me that every little thing a father does with his child in public is noticed and praised, and everything a mother does with her child in public is as unseen and ever-present as the particles of oxygen in the air we breathe. You would tell me that the body repairs, that the wound that has replaced your vulva and vagina, or your caesar scar, will heal, and that you needed to open up like that, layer by layer, to become. You would tell me that your body will not be yours again for many years, and that it's okay to weep for that. You would tell me the act of giving birth is a fire we survive that transforms us from lead to gold, from mortals to martyrs. You would tell me that grief has no end to it, and once I accept that I will also know love has no end, too.

THE FOURTH TRIMESTER

Little Bug

With hot breath I blow
Straight arrow to little bug
Wings from book's pages.

On Becoming

And what of this becoming?
They say a woman is
a mother from the instant
of the child's conception,
a father from the first moment
he holds his child.
But it's not as simple as that,
there is the mother
you had imagined
you would be,
the mother you are,
and the mother
you become through
what you gain
and what you lose
along the way.

An Ode to Women Who Choose Not to Be Mothers

When I was a child
my mother would make
traditional Croatian
juha from beef bones
once a week.
For two hours the pot
would bubble and roll,
the smell of soup penetrating the curtains
and upholstery for the next two days.
A peeled potato, carrots, celery,
flat-leaf parsley, garlic, an onion, whole.
My favourite moment was—
after slurping the broth—fighting over
who would suck the marrow out of the bones.
Flat of a knife, scraping out the marrow
to savour the luscious feel
of the fatty globules
pressed against the roof
of my mouth. The
unctuous texture,
the quiet slide
down the back of
my throat.

A savouring.
Carpe diem.
"Plucking the day"
as Latin scholars would say.
Not 'seizing,' but 'plucking'
those slow moments
of unctuousness
without interruption.
To gather ripening
fruit, fat bunches
of wildflowers in hand
as every woman has the right to,
without having to be the fruit,
be the flower.

Ash

response to the Black Summer bushfires of 2019-20

The memory is like burnt toast,
the smell lingers too long,
in my kitchen, in my house,
seeps into the curtains.
And I don't know what to do to cauterize
this lingering, except to open the curtains,
the blinds, the windows, watch the light filter
through the remnants of ash on the glass,
a film of chalky makeup on its face.

But this play has gone on too long,
the natural light reveals what the stage light
could not; the actor is not happy.
A finger swiped across the outside window
leaves a smear of clarity,
skin exposed to oxygen.
Her vision is no longer frosted,
Medea's mask melts
like cheap foundation in the heat.
The actor is not happy, and she knows
the role she must now play
when she exits stage right.
The dress rehearsal is over
and toast is burning in the kitchen.

Due Preparations for the Plague

'There have been as many plagues as wars in history,
yet always plagues and wars take people by surprise.'—Albert Camus

Enough of beaked mask and burred spherical disease,
of plucked chickens strapped to writhing poxed bodies,
of serpents sliced, rubbed over diseased flesh,
of fresh urine tinctures and ground emerald potions,
of persecuting Jews, travelers, and witches in shadowed alleyways
as we have done for centuries, of the poultice made from human faeces
and public flagellation and God's wrath upon humanity,
of the conjunction of stars and planets presaging plague,
of dead bodies catapulted over walls into the enemy's city,
of placating the four humors of the body;
fire, earth, air, water with hydroxychloroquine,
enough enough enough of doors welded shut
like the mouths of silk road officials, of bleach cures
that whiten the gray areas of the mind, of our mind's
confusion when presented with the facts of science
that smooth our passage through this earth
every single day, enough of the elbow bump of death
while we wait for a 'cure' that—though imperfect—is here, enough,
when the answer lies before us, sitting in our palm
like a fledgling that has fallen out of a tree, looking up,
asking, 'Did you give birth to me?'

Wall

There should be a word
for the unblemished piece
of wall that a painting
used to cover.
There should be a word
for a person who
breaks your
heart with no end,
over and over.
There should be a word
for a child who wants so
desperately to be loved
she disappears into the space
behind that painting.

I Have Used Up All the Feelings

I have used up all
the feelings I had for you.
They're gone.
The hate, the love,
the spite, the regret;
once, they were as
solid as a chunk of
steel-gray concrete.
Now they've disappeared
like flecks of dust
into the air.

There are some things
I know I like:
the afternoon light
filtering through the dune grass,
when the world becomes golden
for a breath or two;
the last of the evening's warm
rays hitting my back;
crisp sea air, the muscles
in my face awakened.

All the time I spent
wanting you to be
one of those things, too.
All the time I spent
thinking and not
feeling my way through.

Papercuts

Papercut on my tongue, the metallic taste of bro-
                                                                                                    ken
                                                                                                words
in my mouth.
The violence in this house is flowering.
Not the purple violets of hurt bodies, but
the spreading yellow-green-blue-black bruises
of hurt words.

I write a letter to my pain, place it
in an envelope to post back to myself
to read in 10 years' time. As I lick the
envelope shut I cut my tongue
on the glutinous edge, bitter gum
sticks, the spit of a lover's kiss
on my parched lips—

Oh madness & pain how you once were my friend!
The friend of Frida, Joni, Plath, Love, all their
daughters & sons (who died, were given away,
& survived)—tore the farmhouse doors off hinges.

Spit mixes in my mouth with the blowtorched edge
of burnt blood. One taste & I know I am done
speaking to you through papercuts and violet words.

When You Need to Start Again

When you need to start again, cut your hair,
dye it red, shave it off, paint it black—
that old hair is no good for you now.

To grow fresh buds of strength,
go out into the field—leave the weeds—
and drink in all the wildflowers within view;
the yellow conostylis,
a pincushion of softness;
the green and red kangaroo paws
bowed in reverence;
the pink-lipped Geraldton wax
never melting in the sun;
a few candles of banksia flowers
that glow, yet never burn.
Then return with your hands
brimming, skin full of pollen, the Westerly
fuming your nose like cheap perfume—
not acrid—dizzy, earthy; full with the promise
of flowers about to puff open.

Then remember he has no power over you now—
the power that was not his to take but yours to give—
whispering into your pillow at night,
'If you leave me, I won't be able to go on'—
that you would ruin him;
that he might die without you;
that you could never sing again without him;
then the next day, honey in hand, muzzling
you, once more, with his rope of words,
'Come on! Sing for me, honey-bee.'

When you need to start again, cut your hair,
dye it red, shave it off, paint it black—
that old hair is no good for you now.
Throw forth your old self, like a worker bee
at the feet of the Queen, wind shaking weeds,
offer up the pollen collected grain by grain to her—
dripping from your hands as honey.
Then feed it to the Queen, tenderly, slowly,
as you sing her a new song,
and watch your hair grow back,
stronger and longer than ever.

(M)OTHER WRITER

I became an invisible writer,
hiding in closets to scribe the labor,
floating dry, ink staining the bathtub.
I cradle wobbly words beside my
newborn's unstable head
on the breastfeeding pillow.
I scratch at my book in the hallway,
tripping over my words, child at my feet.
I tap into my phone in the glow of blue light
under the invisible forcefield
of the blanket on the couch.
I play hide and seek,
scribbling in the space between
the back fence and garden shed.
A sacred workspace in my car,
my son at T-ball practice,
a cone of silence.
McDonald's has free Wi-Fi
and a playground. The pantry
at home becomes a cave
with supplies and quietude,
opening up time and space
to infinity.
Writing noise out of daycare,
preschool and school pick ups.

I have two dissertations in the circular
work of being a writer, cook, cleaner,
student, tutor, teacher, mother, farm-worker,
household manager; in having no boundaries,
losing sleep, nearly drowning,
staying up to write
until the light across the road
in front of the church goes out.

The carved hardwood desk, the view of lilting trees,
filtered light, a wife to bring me sandwiches and tea,
to keep the children at bay so I could write
Other Lies of Great Male Authors and
Writing in a Secluded Cabin in the Woods—
from my walk-in pantry. Aghast with the romance
of the twilight space I create to write my histories;
The Road Out of the Dark of Winter,
Absolving Myself of (M)other-Writer Guilt and
Holding the Thorns Back on the Path, all this work,
all this brushing away of sand for those
who come after me to be seen.

THE HARVEST

All those paintings of peasants bent over in fields,
light streaming through hay bales, sickles held high.

Yet none show the tattooed creases of dirt in heels
the spent hands that form a fist at the end of a day's reaping,

the stench of sweat that steams from the scalp
like an awakening field on a dewy morning.

Legs brown and long as a filly's, a t-shirt tan,
the melanoma that may or may not have been the origins of thyroid cancer.

The paintings don't show how the parents exhort the children
at the dinner table each night to do well at school

so they do not have to bend over in fields culling, gleaning, gathering,
while golden light streams through flowing skirts or reflects off sharpened
knives.

CEMENTERIO (CEMETERY)

after 'Cementerio (Cemetery), Juchitán, Oaxaca'
by Graciela Iturbide

Release the birds
for there is no release
from the gravity of loss
and the weight of the sky.
A pillow word.
A floating woman:
bundle of sticks in hand,
one pointing upwards
like a staff, the
Princess of Pentacles,
unrepentant.
Translation dissolves
into whitewashed walls,
like the gap in meaning
of the word 'time' between
my language and yours.

In a world black and white
walls melt into sky.
Your body is a shadow,
the shape of a womb, or a tomb.
The unsayable remains behind
a wall, or becomes a photograph,
an image no tide could hold back.
Knowledge, a seduction,
like flocks of swallows breathing;
expanding and contracting,
back and forth
in the sea of the air.
Vacant window frames
entrances to other worlds—
a shell broken; a kernel eaten.
A widow wears her
bedclothes inside out,
sleeps with a bundle of sticks,
dreams of a wine-dark
sea of birds.

Statues

When I look at the statues of soldiers, cold brass rifles in hand, chins pointed up to the sky I wonder about those left behind, the ones outside the frame. Mothers raising children alone, feeding scraps to the chickens, sewing school clothes back together with black thread—the only color left in the sewing box—holding their breath for the mailman, the news reel, the rumors passed from lip to lip. Sometimes, in that shadowless sky, by the starlight of a greasy Edison bulb I see my baba with her back against the door of her father's *taverna*, her full weight, her deep-grooved palms pressed into the wood in a kind of backwards prayer. Belly swollen like the incoming tide—husband not yet returned from the front—willing herself not to quiver, or let her eyes tell a story when the German soldiers came through the door. When I was a child, whenever war movies came on TV, she would cover her eyes, thrust the remote at me, insist I change the channel. Her first husband never returned from the war. She raised two children alone, then married my grandfather and had four more. And I wonder where the statues are for those fallen from the light, the ones who survived the tide and left their hearts behind the door; frozen bullet in an unusable gun.

taverna = tavern/pub (Croatian/Greek)

Attributions to the following authors and their work:

The source text for 'The First Month' to 'The Ninth Month' (inclusive) is Heidi Murkoff and Sharon Mazel's *What to Expect When You're Expecting* New York: Workman Pub, 2008.

The source text for 'A Birth' is Emily Wright's *The Sands of My Life* Tales of the Mojave Road Publishing, 1994.

'Night Stitches (A Cento)' contains lines from: 'Night Waitress' by Lynda Hull; 'At Night' by Stanley Plumley; 'Night' by HD; 'At Night' by Yone Noguchi; 'One Night' by Mathias Svalina; Susan Griffin, quoted in Adrienne Rich's *Of Woman Born*; 'The Duirno Elegies' by Rilke; 'Night Seasons' by Stephen Kuusisto; 'Hard Night' by Christian Wiman; and 'Poetry of the Night' by Giannina Braschi.

In 'Raising Demons Among the Savages' the line "And will she come home again?" is from Shirley Jackson's *Life Among the Savages* Penguin, 1953.

The source text for 'On Day One, We Will Begin Working' is Ron Nixon and Linda Qiu's article 'Trump's Evolving Words on the Wall' *The New York Times*, 18 January 2018.

The source text for 'O The Celestial Objects' is the Santa Barbara Astronomy Society information sheet, 2018.

If There is a Butterfly That Drinks Tears
by Natalie Damjanovich-Napoleon

for Brett and Samuel

I would like to acknowledge this collection was written on the unceded lands of the Chumash of Syukhtun/Santa Barbara and the Noongar people of Walyalup/Fremantle. I pay respects to their elders past and present.

With thanks to the KSP Writers' Centre for the residency.

Acknowledgement for poems previously published is made to the following anthologies and journals: *To Give Life a Shape: Poems Inspired by the Santa Barbara Museum of Art Santa Barbara* CA, Gunpowder Press, 2017; *Kaleidoscope: The Colours of Katharine: An Anthology of Short Fiction and Poetry* Perth WA, Wild Weeds Press, 2019; *Mountain Secrets* Port Adelaide SA, Ginninderra Press, 2019; *Poetry d'Amour* Perth WA, WA Poets Publishing, 2019; *Messages From the Embers: Australian Bushfire Poetry Anthology* Sydney NSW, Black Quill Press, 2020; *Australian Poetry Anthology* Melbourne VIC, Australian Poetry Ltd, 2020; *What We Carry: Poetry on Childbearing* Canberra ACT, Recent Work Press, 2021; *Heroines: An Anthology of Short Fiction and Poetry, vol. 4* Wollongong NSW, The Neo Perennial Press, 2022; *Antipodes*, *The Australian* (Review), *Cordite*, *Literary Orphans*, *StylusLit* and *Westerly.*

First published 2023

POETRY

ISBN: 978-0-6456337-5-7

BOOK, TYPSETTING, AND LOGO DESIGN
Mountains Brown Press

PUBLISHER
Life Before Man

Gazebo Books
PO Box 375
Summer Hill
New South Wales 2130
Australia

gazebobooks.com.au

This book was made possible thanks to Anthony Mark Day

COVER IMAGE: *Thing No. 9*, 2019, oil on canvas, 25.5 x 20.5 cm, © Phil Day

www.ingramcontent.com/pod-product-compliance
Lightning Source LLC
LaVergne TN
LVHW051003080826
845145LV00009B/2427

* 9 7 8 0 6 4 5 6 3 3 7 5 7 *